Nate, Let's Skate

Mary Elizabeth Salzmann

Consulting Editor, Diane Craig, M.A./Reading Specialist

ABDO Publishing Company

Published by ABDO Publishing Company, 4940 Viking Drive, Edina, Minnesota 55435.

Printed in the United States.

Credits
Edited by: Pam Price
Curriculum Coordinator: Nancy Tuminelly
Cover and Interior Design and Production: Mighty Media
Photo Credits: AbleStock, Corbis Images, Anders Hanson, Hemera, Photodisc, Wewerka Photography

Library of Congress Cataloging-in-Publication Data

Salzmann, Mary Elizabeth, 1968-
    Nate, let's skate / Mary Elizabeth Salzmann.
       p. cm. -- (First rhymes)
    Includes index.
    ISBN 1-59679-497-6 (hardcover)
    ISBN 1-59679-498-4 (paperback)
       1. English language--Rhyme--Juvenile literature. I. Title. II. Series.

PE1517.S3554 2005
808.1--dc22
                                                                    2005048780

SandCastle™ books are created by a professional team of educators, reading specialists, and content developers around five essential components that include phonemic awareness, phonics, vocabulary, text comprehension, and fluency. All books are written, reviewed, and leveled for guided reading and early intervention reading, and designed for use in shared, guided, and independent reading and writing activities to support a balanced approach to literacy instruction.

Let Us Know

After reading the book, SandCastle would like you to tell us your stories about reading. What is your favorite page? Was there something hard that you needed help with? Share the ups and downs of learning to read. We want to hear from you! To get posted on the ABDO Publishing Company Web site, send us e-mail at:

sandcastle@abdopub.com

SandCastle Level: Beginning

-ate

crate

gate

plate

skate

slate

Here is the  .

See the  .

Here is a  .

Here is the .

This is a  .

The crate is black.

The gate is closed.

The plate is round.

The skate is black.

The slate is flat.

Nate, Let's Skate

Nate, do you want to skate?
From, Kate

In the mail,
Nate got a slate.

Nate, do you want to skate?
From, Kate

The slate
was from Kate.
It said, "Nate,
do you want to skate?"

Nate, do you want [to] [play]?
From, Kate

Nate likes to skate,
so he took the slate
and met Kate
by the gate.

Nate, do you want to skate?
From, Kate

At the gate,
Nate gave Kate
her slate
and a bun on a plate.

After Kate ate,
she put the plate
and the slate
in a crate.

"Thank you, Nate!"
said Kate.

"Now let's skate!"

About SandCastle™

A professional team of educators, reading specialists, and content developers created the SandCastle™ series to support young readers as they develop reading skills and strategies and increase their general knowledge. The SandCastle™ series has four levels that correspond to early literacy development in young children. The levels are provided to help teachers and parents select the appropriate books for young readers.

Emerging Readers
(no flags)

Beginning Readers
(1 flag)

Transitional Readers
(2 flags)

Fluent Readers
(3 flags)

These levels are meant only as a guide. All levels are subject to change.

To see a complete list of SandCastle™ books and other nonfiction titles from ABDO Publishing Company, visit www.abdopub.com or contact us at:
4940 Viking Drive, Edina, Minnesota 55435 • 1-800-800-1312 • fax: 1-952-831-1632